D1128724

Joisien, TX

States

PENNSYLVANIA

by Tyler Maine

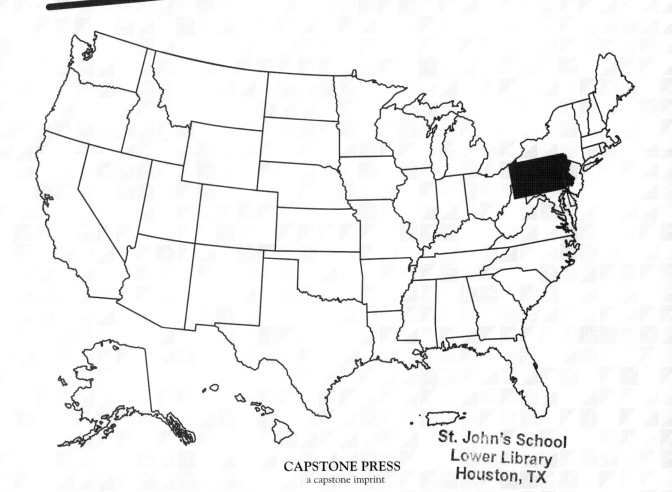

St. John's School
Lower Library
Houston, TX

CAPSTONE PRESS
a capstone imprint

Next Page Books are published by Capstone Press,
1710 Roe Crest Drive, North Mankato, Minnesota 56003
www.mycapstone.com

Copyright © 2017 by Capstone Press, a Capstone imprint. All rights
reserved. No part of this publication may be reproduced in whole or
in part, or stored in a retrieval system, or transmitted in any form
or by any means, electronic, mechanical, photocopying, recording, or
otherwise, without written permission of the publisher.

Library of Congress Cataloging-in-Publication Data
Cataloging-in-publication information is on file with the Library of
Congress.
ISBN 978-1-5157-0425-6 (library binding)
ISBN 978-1-5157-0484-3 (paperback)
ISBN 978-1-5157-0536-9 (ebook PDF)

Editorial Credits
Jaclyn Jaycox, editor; Kazuko Collins and Katy LaVigne, designers;
Morgan Walters, media researcher; Tori Abraham, production specialist

Photo Credits
AP Images: Charles Sykes, middle 19; Capstone Press: Angi Gahler,
map 4, 7; CriaImages.com: Jay Robert Nash Collection, top 18;
iStockphoto: bgwalker, top left 20; Library of Congress: Prints and
Photographs Division Washington, 27; Newscom: Everett Collection,
bottom 18; North Wind Picture Archives, 12, 25, 26; One Mile Up, Inc.,
flag, seal 23; Shutterstock: Aneese, 17, Brandon Alms, bottom left
21, Brent Hofacker, top right 21, dean bertoncelj, bottom 24, Delmas
Lehman, bottom right 8, Dobresum, 28, f11photo, cover, 5, 16, Helga
Esteb, top 19, Henryk Sadura, 13, Jeff Feverston, bottom right 20, John
Barry de Nicola, 29, Jon Bilous, 6, bottom left 8, Lissandra Melo, 11,
LorraineHudgins, middle left 21, Mountain Laurel (Kalmia latifolia),
top right 20, Nagel Photography, 10, photolike, top 24, picturepartners,
14, Pigprox, 9, s_bukley, middle 18, Steve Oehlenschlager, bottom
left 20, Tarasyuk Igor, top left 21, Tom Reichner, middle right
21, Tupungato, 15, Vibe Images, bottom right 21, Zack Frank, 7;
Wikimedia: sleepysmile, bottom 19

All design elements by Shutterstock

Printed and bound in China.
0316/CA21600187
012016   009436F16

TABLE OF CONTENTS

Want to take your research further? Ask your librarian if your school subscribes to PebbleGo Next. If so, when you see this helpful symbol ⟨⟩ throughout the book, log onto www.pebblegonext.com for bonus downloads and information.

LOCATION

Pennsylvania is in the northeastern United States, near the East Coast. New Jersey is on its eastern edge. To the south is Maryland. New York lines the northern border. Pennsylvania's northwest corner faces Lake Erie, while West Virginia bends around Pennsylvania's southwest corner. Ohio lies to the west. Harrisburg is the state capital. Pennsylvania's largest cities are Philadelphia, Pittsburgh, and Allentown.

PebbleGo Next Bonus! To print and label your own map, go to www.pebblegonext.com and search keywords:

PA MAP

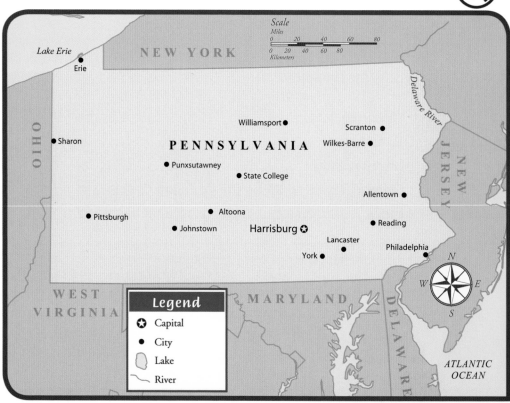

Philadelphia is known as the birthplace of the United States.

GEOGRAPHY

Pennsylvania has a rolling landscape of hills and valleys. The Appalachian Mountains cover most of the state. The Allegheny and Monongahela rivers meet in Pittsburgh to form the Ohio River. Forests cover more than half the state. Pennsylvania's northwestern area has many natural ponds and lakes. Near Lake Erie the land's elevation drops to a lowland plain. Mount Davis is part of the Allegheny Mountains. As the state's highest point, Mount Davis rises 3,213 feet (979 meters) above sea level. Many people enjoy skiing, snowboarding, and snowmobiling in the Pocono Mountains, which are in the eastern part of the state.

To watch a video about Independence Hall and the Liberty Bell, go to www.pebblegonext.com and search keywords:

PA VIDEO

The Susquehanna River is a wide and long river that flows into the Chesapeake Bay.

Hawk Mountain Sanctuary, located in the Appalachian Mountain chain, is the world's first refuge for birds of prey.

Lake Erie

LAKE ERIE PLAIN

Allegheny River

ALLEGHENY PLATEAU

West Branch Susquehanna River

Delaware River

APPALACHIAN MOUNTAINS

ALLEGHENY MOUNTAINS

POCONO MOUNTAINS

Ohio River

Susquehanna River

Juniata River

BLUE MOUNTAINS

PIEDMONT PLATEAU

Monongahela River

APPALACHIAN RIDGE AND VALLEY

ATLANTIC COASTAL PLAIN

APPALACHIAN MOUNTAINS

Mount Davis

Scale
Miles
0   20   40   60   80
0 20 40 60 80
Kilometers

Legend

⌇ Appalachian Trail

▲ Highest Point

⛰ Mountain Area

〰 River

WEATHER

Pennsylvania has cold winters and warm summers. The average January temperature in Pennsylvania is 28 degrees Fahrenheit (minus 2 degrees Celsius). The average July temperature is 69°F (21°C).

Average High and Low Temperatures (Philadelphia, PA)

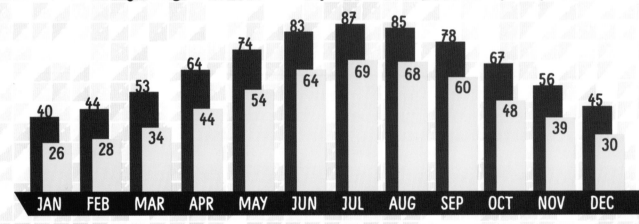

	JAN	FEB	MAR	APR	MAY	JUN	JUL	AUG	SEP	OCT	NOV	DEC
High	40	44	53	64	74	83	87	85	78	67	56	45
Low	26	28	34	44	54	64	69	68	60	48	39	30

LANDMARKS

Independence Hall

The Declaration of Independence and the U.S. Constitution were signed at Independence Hall in Philadelphia.

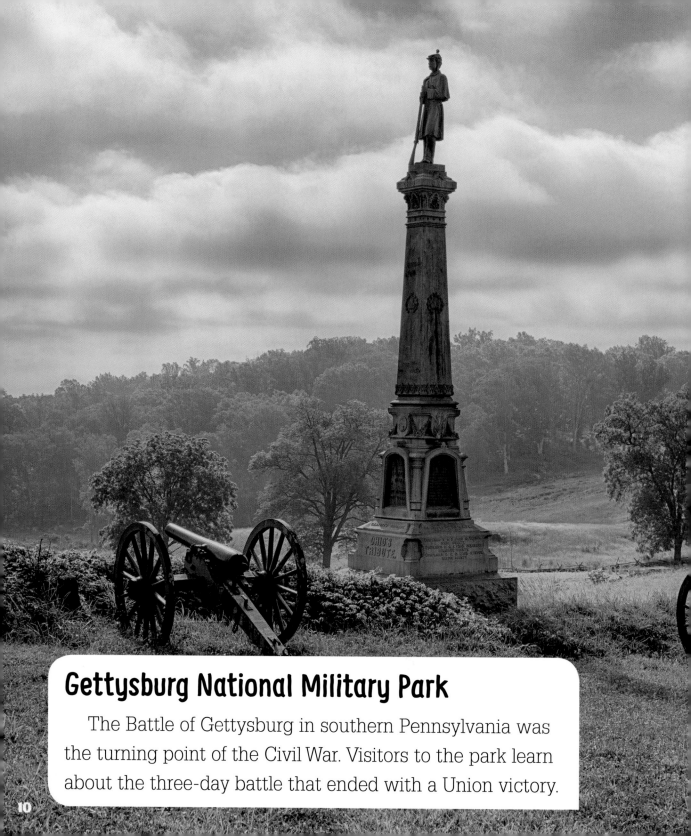

Gettysburg National Military Park

The Battle of Gettysburg in southern Pennsylvania was the turning point of the Civil War. Visitors to the park learn about the three-day battle that ended with a Union victory.

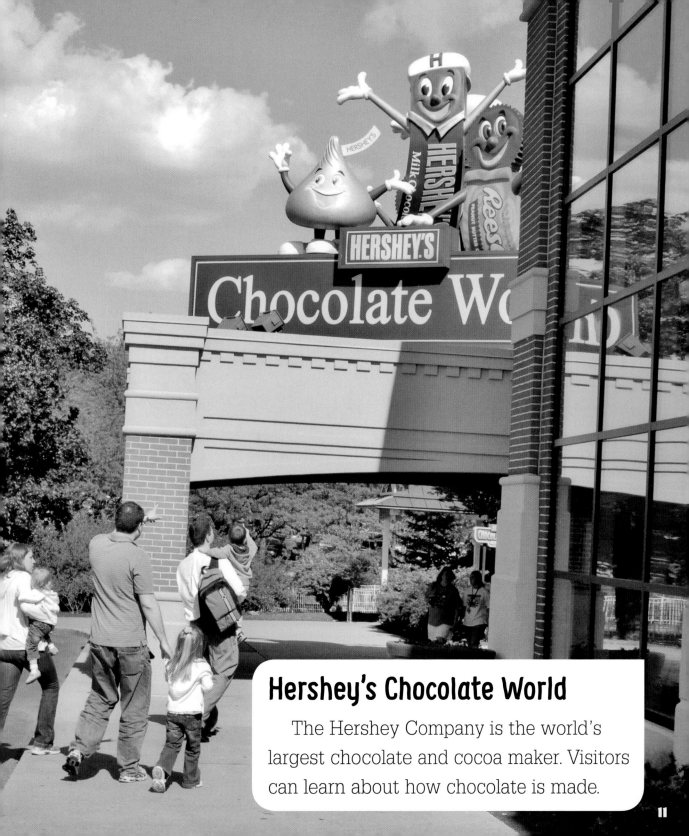

Hershey's Chocolate World

The Hershey Company is the world's largest chocolate and cocoa maker. Visitors can learn about how chocolate is made.

HISTORY AND GOVERNMENT

When Henry Hudson sailed into the Delaware Bay, he claimed land, including Pennsylvania, for the Dutch.

Henry Hudson was probably the first European in Pennsylvania. He sailed into Delaware River Bay in 1609. In 1643 settlers arrived from Sweden. In 1664 the English took over the region. William Penn started a colony in 1681. In 1776 the Declaration of Independence was signed in Philadelphia. In 1783 the colonists won the Revolutionary War against Great Britain. Representatives met in Philadelphia to write a constitution. As soon as a colony accepted the U.S. Constitution, it became a U.S. state. On December 12, 1787, Pennsylvania became the 2nd state.

Pennsylvania has three branches of government. The governor is head of the executive branch, which carries out state laws. The legislative branch is called the General Assembly. It has a 50-member Senate and a 203-member House of Representatives that writes and changes state laws. The supreme court is the highest court in Pennsylvania's judicial branch.

The capitol's dome was inspired by St. Peter's Basilica in Rome and stands at 272 feet (83 m) tall.

INDUSTRY

Pennsylvania is a leading producer of steel for buildings, machines, and the food industry. In recent years, Pennsylvania's steel industry has not been as strong. Pennsylvania's mines produce coal, which is used for heat and electricity. Pennsylvania's trees are also important to the state's economy. Pennsylvania is a large producer of maple syrup. Lumber mills make hardwood lumber and paper products. Furniture and cabinet factories make pieces for homes and businesses. Milk is Pennsylvania's leading farm product. Pennsylvania's rich history, scenic beauty, and outdoor activities bring many tourists to the state.

Mushrooms are a leading crop for Pennsylvania.

The U.S. Steel Tower building in Pittsburgh is the city's tallest skyscraper, reaching 841 feet (256 m) high.

POPULATION

Most Pennsylvanians have European ancestors. They may have come from Germany, Ireland, Italy, England, or Poland. Many Italian families settled in mining and mill towns in Pennsylvania. Today many Italians live in the "Little Italy" area of South Philadelphia. About one of every 10 residents is African-American. Many people of Asian and Hispanic cultures also live in Pennsylvania.

Population by Ethnicity

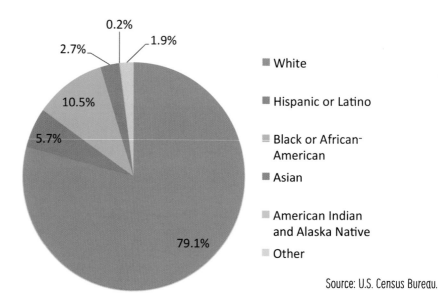

- White
- Hispanic or Latino
- Black or African-American
- Asian
- American Indian and Alaska Native
- Other

0.2%
1.9%
2.7%
10.5%
5.7%
79.1%

Source: U.S. Census Bureau.

FAMOUS PEOPLE

Louisa May Alcott (1832–1888) wrote *Little Women* (1868), *Little Men* (1871), and other books. They told about children growing up in the 1860s. She was born in Philadelphia.

Will Smith (1968–) is a former rapper and now a famous actor. He has starred in *The Fresh Prince of Bel-Air, Ali*, and *Men in Black*. He was born in Philadelphia.

Milton Hershey (1857–1945) opened the Hershey Chocolate Company in 1894. He gave most of his fortune to the Milton Hershey School for Disadvantaged Children.

Tara Lipinski (1982–) won the gold medal in ice skating at the 1998 Olympic Winter Games in Nagano, Japan. She was born in Philadelphia.

Judy Schachner (1951–) wrote the *Skippyjon Jones* series of books. She lives in Swarthmore.

Jerry Spinelli (1941–) wrote the Newbery Award–winning book *Maniac Magee*. He was born in Norristown.

STATE SYMBOLS

Tree

hemlock

Flower

mountain laurel

Bird

ruffed grouse

Fish

brook trout

PebbleGo Next Bonus! To make a Dutch dessert for which Pennsylvania is famous, go to www.pebblegonext.com and search keywords:

PA RECIPE

Beverage

milk

Cookie

chocolate chip

Fossil

Phacops rana

Animal

white-tailed deer

Insect

firefly

Dog

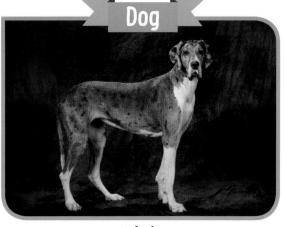

great dane

FAST FACTS

STATEHOOD
1787

CAPITAL ☆
Harrisburg

LARGEST CITY ●
Philadelphia

SIZE
44,743 square miles (115,884 square kilometers) land area (2010 U.S. Census Bureau)

POPULATION
12,773,801 (2013 U.S. Census estimate)

STATE NICKNAME
Keystone State

STATE MOTTO
"Virtue, Liberty, and Independence"

PebbleGo Next Bonus!
To learn the lyrics to the state song, go to www.pebblegonext.com and search keywords:

STATE SEAL

Pennsylvania's seal was adopted by the General Assembly in 1791. Like the state flag, the seal shows an eagle perched on top of a shield. The ship, plow, and wheat on the seal represent the state's commerce, resources, and agriculture. An Indian cornstalk and an olive branch rise up from beneath the shield.

PebbleGo Next Bonus!
To print and color your own flag, go to www.pebblegonext.com and search keywords:

PA FLAG

STATE FLAG

Pennsylvania's flag was first approved in 1799. The flag shows the Pennsylvania Coat of Arms. The coat of arms has two black horses supporting a shield. An eagle stands on top of the shield, and an olive branch and a cornstalk are crossed below it. Pennsylvania's motto, "Virtue, Liberty, and Independence," is printed on a ribbon below the shield.

MINING PRODUCTS

coal, natural gas, limestone, portland cement

MANUFACTURED GOODS

chemicals, food products, metals, machinery, electronic equipment

FARM PRODUCTS

potatoes, mushrooms, soybeans, apples, corn

PROFESSIONAL SPORTS TEAMS

Philadelphia 76ers (NBA)
Philadelphia Eagles (NFL)
Pittsburgh Steelers (NFL)
Philadelphia Flyers (NHL)
Pittsburgh Penguins (NHL)
Philadelphia Phillies (MLB)
Pittsburgh Pirates (MLB)

PENNSYLVANIA TIMELINE

1600s — Shawnee, Lenni Lenape, and other American Indian tribes are living in the Pennsylvania area.

1620 — The Pilgrims establish a colony in the New World in present-day Massachusetts.

1643 — Swedish colonists settle on Tinicum Island.

1681 — The Pennsylvania area is given to William Penn.

1776 The Declaration of Independence is signed in Philadelphia.

1776 On July 8 the Liberty Bell is rung to celebrate the first public reading of the Declaration of Independence.

1787 On December 12 Pennsylvania becomes the 2nd U.S. state.

1812 Harrisburg becomes the state capital.

1861–1865 The Union and the Confederacy fight the Civil War. Pennsylvania fights with the Union.

1863 From July 1–3 the Battle of Gettysburg is fought in southern Pennsylvania during the Civil War.

1889 On May 31 the Johnstown Flood kills 2,209 people.

1914–1918 World War I is fought; the United States enters the war in 1917.

1939 Frank Lloyd Wright finishes construction of Fallingwater near Mill Run.

1939–1945 World War II is fought; the United States enters the war in 1941.

1957 Pennsylvania's first nuclear power plant begins producing electricity.

1979 The Three Mile Island nuclear reactor accident occurs in Dauphin County. The accident brings about big changes in U.S. nuclear power plant safety.

2001 United Airlines Flight 93 crashes near Shanksville on September 11 after passengers confront terrorists who took control of the plane. It is one of four flights taken over by terrorists that day. Nearly 3,000 people are killed in the attacks.

2003 On January 24 Pennsylvania governor Tom Ridge becomes the first secretary of the U.S. Department of Homeland Security.

2006 More than 200,000 people are evacuated from homes in the Wilkes-Barre area because of flooding.

2010 Pennsylvania makes casino gambling legal.

2015 An Amtrak train derails in Philadelphia while traveling at twice the speed limit; eight people are killed and more than 200 are injured.

Glossary

ancestor *(AN-ses-tuhr)*—a member of a person's family who lived a long time ago

census *(SEN-suhss)*—an official count of all the people living in a country or district

commerce *(KOM-urss)*—the buying and selling of things in order to make money

descend *(dee-SEND)*—if you are descended from someone, you belong to a later generation of the same family

evacuate *(i-VA-kyuh-wayt)*—to leave an area during a time of danger

executive *(ig-ZE-kyuh-tiv)*—the branch of government that makes sure laws are followed

immigrant *(IM-uh-gruhnt)*—someone who comes from abroad to live permanently in a country

industry *(IN-duh-stree)*—a business which produces a product or provides a service

judicial *(joo-DISH-uhl)*—to do with the branch of government that explains and interprets the laws

legislature *(LEJ-iss-lay-chur)*—a group of elected officials who have the power to make or change laws for a country or state

nuclear *(NOO-klee-ur)*—power created by splitting atoms

Read More

Ganeri, Anita. *United States of America: A Benjamin Blog and His Inquisitive Dog Guide.* Country Guides. Chicago: Heinemann Raintree, 2015.

Marciniak, Kristin. *What's Great About Pennsylvania?* Our Great States. Minneapolis: Lerner Publications Company, 2014.

Waring, Kerry Jones. *Pennsylvania.* It's My State! New York: Cavendish Square Publishing, 2014.

Internet Sites

FactHound offers a safe, fun way to find Internet sites related to this book. All of the sites on FactHound have been researched by our staff.

Here's all you do:

Visit *www.facthound.com*

Type in this code: 9781515704256

Check out projects, games and lots more at
www.capstonekids.com

Critical Thinking Using the Common Core

1. Which Great Lake touches Pennsylvania in its northwest corner? (Key Ideas and Details)

2. Which of the three Pennsylvania landmarks listed in this book would you most like to visit and why? (Integration of Knowledge and Ideas)

3. What battle was the turning point of the Civil War? (Key Ideas and Details)

Index